Seymour And Friends

Written by
Phyllis Bechtold

Illustrated by
Royce Vaughn

Arnica Publishing, Choteau, MT

Special Thanks

A special thanks to my family and friends
for their support and encouragement.

And to my illustrator, Royce, who makes my projects
happen in an easy and pleasant way...

2016 - ARNICA PUBLISHING • Choteau, MT

contents

About Birding 1-2
Americian Goldfinch 3-4
American Robin 5-6
Blue Bird 7-8
Tuffted Titmouse 9-10
Northern Mockingbird 11-12
Northern Cardinal 13-14
Black Capped Chickadee 15-16
Killdeer 17-18
Barn Swallow 19-20
Meadowlark 21-22
American Bald Eagle 23-24
Downy Woodpecker 25-26
Yellow Throated Warbler 27-28
Hummingbird 29-30

Bluejay 31-32
Red-Breasted Nuthatch 33-34
House Wren 35-36
Cedar Waxwing 37-38
Song Sparrow 39-40
Magpie 41-42
American Crow 43-44
Red-Winged Blackbird 45-46
House Finch 47-48
Northern Flicker 49-50
Morning Dove 51-52
Evening Grosbeak 53-54
Facts About Birding 55
About the Author 56

About Birding

Fresh air, exercise and the wonders of nature all combine to make birding one of the best outdoor activities for both children and adults. You don't need special equipment…just your eyes, ears and a love for the outdoors. Birds are everywhere…in cities, parks, meadows, barns, forests and more.

Nature is a part of who we are. We do not live alone on this earth. We are part of a bigger place…nature. Look around and become more observant as you look for the birds in this book. Listen to the calls and identify the species. Make note of where you are when you see these birds.
Note their beauty and graceful flight.

Be thankful for the beauty of nature that is all around you.

I am Seymour Bluffs, an American Bald Eagle. I am so named because I have a very sharp eyesight and can see more than most birds. I have a white head and white tail feathers. I live mostly in Alaska and along the Mississippi and Missouri Rivers and the seacoasts. I need tall trees in which to build my nest and open water where I can fish for my food. I am quite a large bird with a wingspan of 6 to 8 feet. My younger siblings have brown heads and tails until they are about 4 to 5 years old. I can fly up to 40 m.p.h. and when I see something that I want to eat, I can fly even faster at up to 140 m.p.h. I like to sit in the tree tops waiting for an easy meal.

I have many feathered friends and want to introduce them to you.

American Goldfinch

What is that bright flash of yellow
That I see along the meadow?
With it's tiny black cap
and black-tipped wings,
Sounds of lively trills and swee!
It's call --a delightful per-chick-o-reee!

- Goldfinches are small birds of about 5 inches.

- The male is a bright yellow in the summer and more drab in the winter.

- The female is duller yellow or olive overall.

- The American Goldfinch is often seen at feeders that offer black oil sunflower or thistle seed.

- Also seen along roadsides, streamsides, open woods, fields and grasslands.

Where I saw this bird:
_____
_____
_____
_____
_____

What was the bird doing?
_____
_____
_____
_____
_____

Date I saw this bird:
_____

American Robin

You'll know that it's Spring
When you hear the Robin sing
"Cheerily cheer-up cheerio"!

The grass is turning green
After a long winter's sleep
And the Robin is hunting
For an earthworm to eat!

- At 10 inches in length the Robin is a standard for measuring other birds -- "larger or smaller than a Robin".

- The Robin is gray-brown above with a darker head and tail, yellow bill with brick red underparts and a white lower belly.

- The Robin is a welcome sight when it's cheery song is the first sign that Spring has arrived.

- You'll see the American Robin in open woodlands, yards, fields and city parks.

- It's favorite food is earthworms and will also feed on insects, spiders, some fruits and berries.

Where I saw this bird:
_____
_____
_____
_____
_____

What was the bird doing?
_____
_____
_____
_____
_____

Date I saw this bird:
_____

Blue Bird

Oh Bluebird friend,
How happy I am,
That you are in my sight
You are such a delight!

- The bluebird is a traditional symbol of happiness

- The bluebird is about 7 inches in length

- The Eastern Bluebird is brilliant blue in color with a red-orange breast

- The Mountain Bluebird has a paler blue to whitish breast and underwing.

- Bluebirds are cavity nesters and prefer nest boxes with an open yard or meadow for easy feeding.

- Bluebirds prefer worms and insects, but can survive on fruits and berries.

Where I saw this bird:
_____
_____
_____
_____
_____

What was the bird doing?
_____
_____
_____
_____
_____

Date I saw this bird:
_____

Tufted Titmouse

If you see an upside-down bird
The chances are, you know
That it's a Tufted Titmouse
Foraging for food while on the go!

- About 6 ½ inches long, the Tufted Titmouse is gray on the back with a whitish breast

- The most unmistakable characteristic of this bird is it's pointed tufted crest upon the top of it's head

- Tufted Titmouse are commonly found in deciduous woodlands, parks, suburbs and at feeders

- It's typical song is a loud whistled "peter, peter, peter"

- You will see the Tufted Titmouse moving down a tree limb or fence post head first -- thus, the upside-down bird!

- Is omnivorous (eats many kinds of foods) but prefers berries.

Where I saw this bird:
_____
_____
_____
_____
_____

What was the bird doing?
_____
_____
_____
_____
_____

Date I saw this bird:
_____

Northern Mockingbird

**Repeating a song of another bird
Is a common trait
Of the Northern Mockingbird!**

- About 10 inches long

- Slender gray birds with white patches on the long tail feathers and wings

- Will come to feeders, but likes insects, spiders and small crustaceans best.

- Often sings at night, imitating other bird's songs

Where I saw this bird:
_____
_____
_____
_____

What was the bird doing?
_____
_____
_____
_____
_____

Date I saw this bird:
_____

Northern Cardinal

My friend the Northern Cardinal
Is feathered all in red,
With a bright red bill
And a crest upon his head!

- The Cardinal is 7 - 9 inches long

- It's song is "birdie, birdie, birdie"

- The female's colors are more muted buff, brown or olive

- The Cardinal's favorite food is black oil sunflower seed.

- You'll see cardinals in low bushes, thickets and back yards

Where I saw this bird:
_____
_____
_____
_____
_____

What was the bird doing?
_____
_____
_____
_____
_____

Date I saw this bird:
_____

Black Capped Chickadee

Oh, if you could see a Chickadee,
Hopping around and singing cheerily,
So entertaining and endearing is he,
As he calls out his name, "chickadee dee,dee"!

- The Chickadee's black cap is his most identifying characteristic on his 5 ½ inch body

- He also has a black bib, black eyes and a pointed black bill over a gray-to-buff body color.

- Chickadees like to eat insects, seeds, grains, and berries. At feeders, they prefer black oil sunflower seeds.

- The Chickadee is part of the Titmouse family so you'll sometimes see it feeding upside down.

Where I saw this bird:

_____
_____
_____
_____
_____

What was the bird doing?

_____
_____
_____
_____
_____

Date I saw this bird:

_____

Killdeer

If a Killdeer's nest is challenged
It's funny what you'll see
In order for her to save the eggs
She'll fake an injury!

- About 10 inches long

- Forages on the ground for insects, invertebrates and some seeds

- Nests on the ground in the open: the nests are shallow and lined with gravel.

- Orange-brown on the back and tail with two distinct breast bands on it's white breast

- The Killdeer likes open ground, plowed fields and pastures often near water

- After faking an injury to deter predators, the adult killdeer will suddenly fly away.

Where I saw this bird:

_____
_____
_____
_____
_____

What was the bird doing?

_____
_____
_____
_____

Date I saw this bird:

_____

Barn Swallow

The aerobatic Barn Swallow
Is dazzling in his flight
As he turns and dips to carefully follow
His food supply into the night!

- About 7 inches in length

- Shiny slate gray to black feathers on the back with reddish-brown underparts

- The Barn Swallows most identifying characteristic is it's deeply forked tail.

- Barn Swallows are sociable and often travel in flocks

- You might see them sitting on a wire waiting for their next meal to fly by

- They like open country near barns, bridges or other buildings.

Where I saw this bird:

_____
_____
_____
_____
_____

What was the bird doing?

_____
_____
_____
_____
_____

Date I saw this bird:

_____

Meadowlark

Both Eastern and Western Meadowlarks
Have a common V
Upon their breasts of yellow-orange
In bold black for you to see!

- About 9 inches long

- Ground feeders of insects, spiders, grains and seeds

- Speckled brown back with yellow throat and breast

- Dark and white stripes on the head

- White outer tail feathers

- Meadowlarks like grassy fields and meadows.

Where I saw this bird:
_____
_____
_____
_____
_____

What was the bird doing?
_____
_____
_____
_____
_____

Date I saw this bird:
_____

American Bald Eagle

He soars along the waters
And sits in trees up high,
He helps her tend their nest
And stays with her for life.

He's the greatest of the raptors,
The Bald Eagle rates up high,
He is the symbol of our nation,
As he reaches for the sky.

- Female eagles are larger than males
- Eagles make shrill, high pitched twittering sounds
- Bald eagles live mostly along open water like rivers, coastlines and lakes
- Bald eagles feed mostly on fish, but also like carrion (dead and decaying flesh)
- An eagle's eyesight is at least four times as sharp as a human's
- The average lifespan of an eagle is 15-20 years

Where I saw this bird:
_____
_____
_____
_____

What was the bird doing?
_____
_____
_____
_____

Date I saw this bird:
_____

Downy Woodpecker

The Downy Woodpecker you'll likely see
Drumming away on the limb of a tree
He's looking for insects or calling a mate
I'm sure he'll not have long to wait!

- Downy Woodpeckers are about 6 inches in length

- Normally, you will hear a drumming sound as they peck on wood, but occasionally will make a "pik" sound.

- Females do not have the red splash of color on the back of their heads

- You'll find the Downy in wooded areas including parks and yards.

- Downys will eat seeds and suet at feeders

Where I saw this bird:
_____
_____
_____
_____
_____

What was the bird doing?
_____
_____
_____
_____

Date I saw this bird:
_____

Yellow Throated Warbler

Of all the warbler family
The one that you might see
Is the Yellow Throated Warbler
With it's song of "witchity, witchity, witchity"!

- About 5 inches long

- Plain gray back with a large white patch on the side of it's head and a gray to white belly

- The male has a mask around it's eyes like that of a raccoon. The female does not have the mask.

- Both male and female have a yellow throat and breast

- Their songs are surprisingly loud and rapid

- They like forest with tall trees

Where I saw this bird:
_____
_____
_____
_____
_____

What was the bird doing?
_____
_____
_____
_____
_____

Date I saw this bird:
_____

Hummingbird

The ruby-throated hummingbird
And it's black-chinned counterpart
Are favorites to watch
As they hover and dart
Around a flower or feeder
With SWEET nectar -- not tart!

- Hummingbirds are very light weight -- about the weight of 3 paperclips!

- Hummingbirds can hover in place, fly up, down, sideways, and backwards.

- Their wings beat at 50-70 times per minute

- Humingbirds have just one very flexible joint at their shoulder that joins their wings to their bodies

- They have very tight feathers of iridescent green and red

- The ruby-throated is the most common in Eastern U.S. and Canada

- The black-chinned is most common in the West and Southwest

Where I saw this bird:

_____
_____
_____
_____
_____

What was the bird doing?

_____
_____
_____
_____
_____

Date I saw this bird:

_____

Bluejay

"Jay, jay, jay" is what you will hear
As this mischievous bird forays so near.
It's bright black eyes and sharp black beaks
It uses for thieving as havoc it wreaks!

- Blue Jays and Stellar's Jays are mischievous and thieving birds at feeders, picnic areas and camps.

- The Blue Jays are pretty birds with bright blue feathers on their back and a white breast. They have a blue crest on their head and white patches on their wings and long tails. Stellar's Jays are dark blue and black overall.

- They will eat nuts, large seeds, some insects and even other bird's eggs and hatchlings.

- The Jay family usually travels in raucous flocks that defend their territory by diving directly at the enemy.

Where I saw this bird:
_____
_____
_____
_____

What was the bird doing?
_____
_____
_____
_____

Date I saw this bird:
_____

Red-Breasted Nuthatch

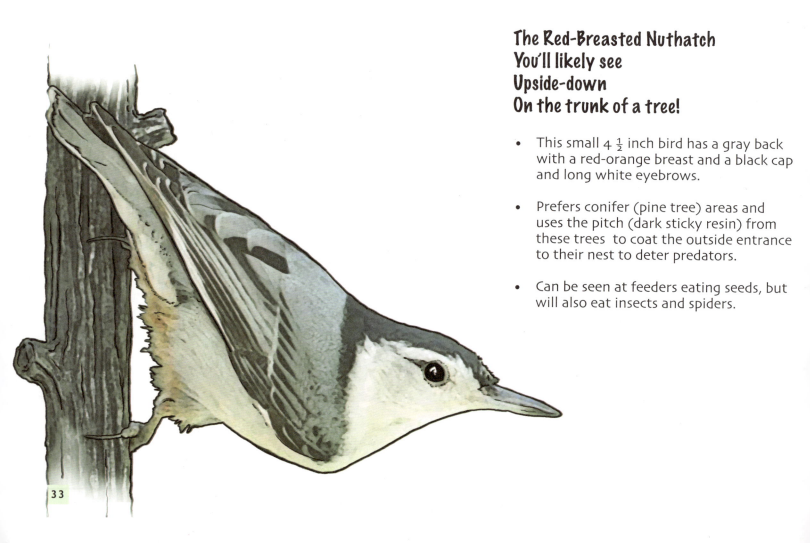

The Red-Breasted Nuthatch
You'll likely see
Upside-down
On the trunk of a tree!

- This small 4 ½ inch bird has a gray back with a red-orange breast and a black cap and long white eyebrows.

- Prefers conifer (pine tree) areas and uses the pitch (dark sticky resin) from these trees to coat the outside entrance to their nest to deter predators.

- Can be seen at feeders eating seeds, but will also eat insects and spiders.

Where I saw this bird:
_____
_____
_____
_____
_____

What was the bird doing?
_____
_____
_____
_____
_____

Date I saw this bird:
_____

House Wren

**The bubbly whistling song of the wren
Will always let you know just when
Winter has gone
And spring has come again!**

- The wren is found all over the lower 48 states.

- Gray/brown from head to tail with lighter under belly

- The wren carries it's tail almost vertical to it's body

- The wren is 4-5 inches in length

- The Wren eats small insects and bugs

Where I saw this bird:
_____
_____
_____
_____
_____

What was the bird doing?
_____
_____
_____
_____
_____

Date I saw this bird:
_____

cedar waxwing

**An orchard field of berries
Is where you'll likely see
A sleekly feathered waxwing
Whistling a high pitched "zeeee!"**

- Waxwings are about 7 inches long

- Found in open woods, orchards, parks and gardens

- Waxwings eat mostly berries, but will also eat sap, flowers and insects

- It's bright yellow tipped tail is a distinguishing mark along with it's red-tipped wings

- The waxwing is a warm brown in color and has a pale yellow belly. It has a pointed crest upon it's head and black eye mask.

Where I saw this bird:
_____
_____
_____
_____
_____

What was the bird doing?
_____
_____
_____
_____
_____

Date I saw this bird:
_____

song sparrow

A large brown center spot
On this bird's streaked chest.
Is the Common Song Sparrow's
Identifying crest!

- Most common sparrow in the United States

- Sings a routine "sweet, sweet, sweet" followed by a trill

- About 6 inches long, brown streaked on top with a white and brown streaked breast

- The song sparrow pumps it's tail up and down as it flies

- Usually found in brushy areas looking for insects and spiders, but will come to feeders for seeds and berries.

Where I saw this bird:
_____
_____
_____
_____
_____

What was the bird doing?
_____
_____
_____
_____
_____

Date I saw this bird:
_____

Magpie

Long sweeping tail of iridescent green
All black and white and very often seen
In rangelands and foothills, on feeders with grain
The gregarious Magpie is never mundane!

- Magpies are large (19 inches in length) black birds with a white chest and a long sweeping iridescent tail

- You might see Magpies on fences along roads or on feeders near ranches often near water.

- The most famous Magpies were the cartoon characters "Heckle and Jeckle" of the 1960's and 70's.

Where I saw this bird:
_____
_____
_____
_____
_____

What was the bird doing?
_____
_____
_____
_____
_____

Date I saw this bird:
_____

42

American Crow

From sea to shining sea
and meadow lands to mountains
You'll see a crow most anywhere,
Sometimes even a public square!

- About 17 inches in length

- Shiny black in color

- Omnivorous (Will eat anything edible)

- Do not mistake the Crow for the Raven that is much larger (24 inches in length) and has a wedge-shaped tail in flight

Where I saw this bird:

_____
_____
_____
_____
_____

What was the bird doing?

_____
_____
_____
_____

Date I saw this bird:

_____

Red-Winged Blackbird

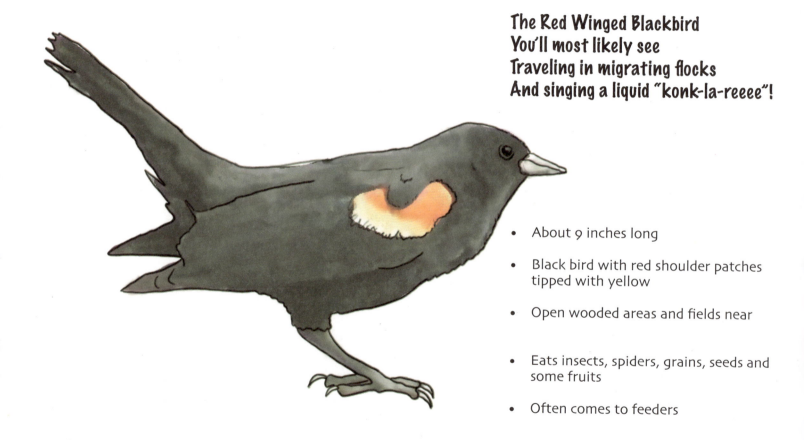

The Red Winged Blackbird
You'll most likely see
Traveling in migrating flocks
And singing a liquid "konk-la-reeee"!

- About 9 inches long

- Black bird with red shoulder patches tipped with yellow

- Open wooded areas and fields near

- Eats insects, spiders, grains, seeds and some fruits

- Often comes to feeders

Where I saw this bird:
_____
_____
_____
_____
_____

What was the bird doing?
_____
_____
_____
_____
_____

Date I saw this bird:
_____

House Finch

A splash of redish orange
On his bib, rump and head!
"Wheat, wheat, wheat" is his call
that you'll often hear on a farmstead

- About 6 inches in length

- Likes feeders and inhabited areas with water

- Adult females and juveniles are brown-streaked overall

- Young males acquire full adult coloring by first fall.

Where I saw this bird:
_____
_____
_____
_____
_____

What was the bird doing?
_____
_____
_____
_____
_____

Date I saw this bird:
_____

Northern Flicker

When you hear a "whicker, whicker, whicker",
Or a "kekekekekekeke",
You'll see a Northern Flicker
on the side of a tree!

- About 12 inches in length
- Found in wooded and suburban areas.
- Prefers ants and insects along with some seeds, grains and berries.
- The "Yellow-Shafted Flicker" is more commonly found in the East and far North.
- The "Red-Shafted Flicker" is more common in the West

Where I saw this bird:
_____
_____
_____
_____

What was the bird doing?
_____
_____
_____
_____

Date I saw this bird:
_____

Morning Dove

**A mournful "oowoo-woo-woo-woo"
Is the sound of a Mourning Dove
Calling to you, you, you!**

- About 12 inches in length and slimmer than a pigeon

- It has a long tail that tapers to a point and has white border during flight

- Brownish pink in color

- Doves are seed and fruit eaters

- You can hear Doves take flight as their wings produce a fluttering whistle

Where I saw this bird:

_____
_____
_____
_____
_____

What was the bird doing?

_____
_____
_____
_____

Date I saw this bird:

_____

Evening Grosbeak

If you've ever seen a Grosbeak
One thing that is for sure,
The part that makes them really neat
Is the large bill for him and her!

- About 8 inches long

- This bird is a large finch with a large strong bill that enables it to crack open seeds and nuts to eat.

- Originally dwellers in the Western Mountains, birdfeeders may have attributed to the expansion of this bird's range

- The Evening Grosbeak has a body of dark yellow with patches of black and white on it's wings.

- One identifying feature is the distinct yellow stripe above it's large bill. The stripe varies to white in the winter.

- Grosbeaks eat seeds, nuts, insects, and small fruit.

Where I saw this bird:
_____
_____
_____
_____
_____

What was the bird doing?
_____
_____
_____
_____

Date I saw this bird:
_____

FACTS ABOUT BIRDING

- Birdwatching connects people with nature
- There are over 800 species of birds in North America
- Birds are everywhere...in your own backyard, park, range, forest or city.
- Birding connects people across generations.
- Birding can be either a social or solitary activity...either way your mind settles down, your senses open up and all of nature becomes your friend.
- You don't need any special equipment to begin birding, but you might like a pair of binoculars and this book to help you get started.

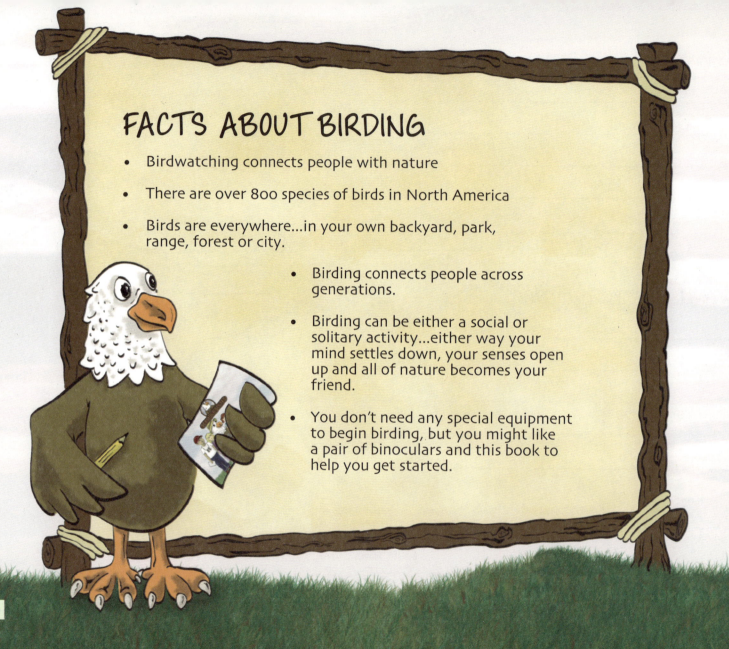

About the Author:

Born in Alton, IL, Phyllis Bechtold's love of nature began early as she grew up on a farm in rural Godfrey, IL. Her love for birdwatching began as a gift of a feeder from her daughters. When she moved back to her family farm and was surrounded by trees, birds and animals her appreciation bloomed.

Seymour Bluffs was created in 2006 for her first book, SEYMOUR BLUFFS AND THE LEGEND OF THE PIASA BIRD.

Her second book soon followed..SEYMOUR BLUFFS AND ROBERT WADLOW. While working and healing on a towboat on the Mississippi, she wrote SEYMOUR BLUFFS THE TOWBOAT HERO.

This book, SEYMOUR AND FRIENDS, has been a work in progress for several years...just sitting in her computer...waiting for the right time.
It is now...

Phyllis Bechtold
8008 Walsh Rd., Godfrey, IL. 62035
(618) 466-1442
seymourbluffs1@gmail.com

Seymour And Friends /Phyllis Bechtold

978-0-9728538-5-9

First published in 2016 by
Arnica Publishing, Choteau, MT
Printed in USA